pocket posh®
left brain/right brain

(50) PUZZLES TO CHANGE
THE WAY YOU THINK

pocket posh®
left brain/right brain

(50) **PUZZLES TO CHANGE THE WAY YOU THINK**

The Puzzle Society™
puzzlesociety.com

Andrews McMeel
Publishing®

Kansas City • Sydney • London

POCKET POSH®
LEFT Brain/RIGHT Brain

Andrews McMeel Publishing, LLC
an Andrews McMeel Universal company
1130 Walnut Street, Kansas City, Missouri 64106

www.andrewsmcmeel.com
www.puzzlesociety.com

This title is published by arrangement with
Eddison Sadd Editions Limited, London.

Text by Charles Phillips

15 16 17 18 19 SHZ 10 9 8 7 6

ISBN: 978-1-4494-0344-7

Illustration © Susie Ghahremani/boygirlparty.com

ATTENTION: SCHOOLS AND BUSINESSES
Andrews McMeel books are available at quantity discounts with bulk
purchase for educational, business, or sales promotional use. For information,
please e-mail the Andrews McMeel Publishing Special Sales Department:
specialsales@amuniversal.com.

introduction

Do you notice the detail but miss the big picture? Are you happier dealing with one thing at a time, or do you have a gift for seeing and making sense of many contributing factors at once?

Studies suggest that your upper brain's left hemisphere foregrounds detail and governs sequential activities, while its right hemisphere provides awareness of the background and spatial relations.

Two Brains? The two hemispheres are often described simply as your "left brain" and "right brain." They are "cross-wired": The left one controls the right side of the body and the right commands the body's left side. At one time the differences in their functioning were thought to be much greater than they are today.

Research led by Professor Robert Ornstein in the 1960s in San Francisco, California, used an EEG (electroencephalography) machine to measure electrical activity in the brains of experimental subjects and suggested that the subjects were more active in the left brain when doing mathematics and more active in the right brain when matching colors.

The left-brain/right-brain theory developed, according to which the left brain was dominant in analytical and rational thinking and the right brain was particularly involved in visual–spatial perception and in creative tasks.

Left Brain, Right Brain—or Whole Brain? Popular writers took up the story. They suggested that people could typically be divided into either left-brain or right-brain thinkers—those who were more adept at logic and mathematics were left-brain, while people with primary skills in art and creativity were right-brain types.

Nowadays, scientists emphasize that most thinking involves many parts of the brain working together simultaneously. Complex mental activities are never entirely isolated in one part of the brain. Nevertheless, the scientists maintain that the upper brain's two sides do have specialized functions and approaches. Left brain/right brain may have been an exaggeration, but it contained a core of truth. Research indicates that to be at our best we need to try to use the whole brain.

Sense of Connection An intriguing recent theory suggests that there was once a time when we did use the whole brain. Right and left brains worked in harmony. Moreover, we all share a faint cultural memory of this, of a tantalizing lost perfection and ease of functioning, and this lies behind religious narratives and myths describing an expulsion from Paradise or fall from a state of perfection. The theory goes that, in most of us, thinking is dominated by the analytical processes typically associated with the left brain, and these tend to make us feel fearful, anxious, and separate from one another. Our perception of separateness leads us to think that we should fight for pre-eminence and resources, and to believe that we can find happiness by achieving success at the expense of others. But we could regain calm and a sense of connection to other people and to our surroundings by learning once again to think with the whole brain.

Paradise Lost? The book *Left in the Dark*, by Graham Gynn and Tony Wright, argues that early human beings experienced an amazing growth in brain functioning and that this was driven by a hormonal mechanism that relied on a tropical fruit diet. When we left the tropical forest—our so-called "Garden of Eden"—and abandoned this diet, the change led to hormonal shifts that damaged the functioning of the brain's left hemisphere.

Two Kinds of Meaning?

When we're talking, we rely on intonation and tone as well as on words to convey meaning. Brain research indicates that while the left brain processes the literal meaning of words, the right brain is at work when we note and interpret a person's intonation. As an example, imagine I write a play in which Cary says "I'm playing in the concert," and Rosalind replies "You're playing?" If her line is said with emphasis on the first word (*You're* playing?), the implication is that she is surprised that Cary, and not someone else, is playing, whereas emphasis on the second word (You're *playing*?) indicates her surprise that he is playing rather than being involved in some other way (as conductor, perhaps?).

According to Gynn and Wright, the right hemisphere was largely unaltered but, as part of these changes, the left hemisphere became dominant. Mystic religious activities such as meditation developed as methods for dampening down activities typically associated with the left brain and reconnecting with the right brain. Their book suggests we can use similar techniques tailored to boost typically right-brain activities to balance our thinking in order to improve our functioning.

Artistic Scientists and Scientific Artists The greatest achievers in the history of science and the arts appear to have built their success on a capacity to use thinking processes associated with both sides of the brain. Take Pablo Picasso, who was clearly able to express in

Retrain Your Brain?

The experience of American neuroscientist Jill Bolte Taylor appears to support Gynn and Wright's position (see main text). In 1996 she had a stroke in her brain's cerebral cortex that severely damaged her powers of cognitive thought. But over eight years she retrained her brain and made a full recovery. Describing the experience in her remarkable book, *My Stroke of Insight* (2009), she reports that she retreated into her upper brain's right hemisphere and rebuilt damaged parts of the left hemisphere. She says that she feels more connected to the world as a result of her experience.

geometric form in his notebooks the artistic work he was doing in his paintings. Centuries earlier, and even more astonishingly, Leonardo da Vinci displayed typically left-brain abilities in mathematics and logical thinking that matched or even exceeded the typically right-brain abilities in visual–spatial thinking that he exhibited as an artist. The painter of *The Last Supper* and the *Mona Lisa* also created many remarkable inventions, including a steam cannon and various pumps, and even produced designs for flying machines—centuries before people took to the air.

It's also said that Albert Einstein had the flash of insight that lay behind his "Theory of Relativity" not when he was laboring over an experiment, but while he was relaxing in the sunshine and speculating about how it would be to move along a sunbeam. He took this intuitive, visual–spatial right-brain insight back to the laboratory and worked it out theoretically using rigorous left-brain scientific methodology.

How to Use This Book For our purposes, the left-brain/right-brain distinction is an easy and fun way to characterize different aspects of our mental processing. It helps you identify your strengths and balance your thinking. To get the most out of the book, first take the Left/Right Test on pages 7–13, and check your responses against the list on page 14. This will determine whether you are stronger in typically left-brain activities or in typically right-brain ones.

Then you have a choice of paths: a left-brain path, with puzzles that particularly test and develop your eye for detail and logic, alongside your numerical and linguistic skills, and a right-brain path, with puzzles and exercises that develop your spatial and visual awareness and ability to think creatively. The aim is to balance your thinking. If you

5

score highly in the right-brain questions in our thinking test, take the left-brain path to develop your logical–numerical skills and your eye for detail. Likewise, if you score highly in the left-brain questions, take the right-brain path to develop your visual–creative skills. If you score equally in each, do all the puzzles!

Each puzzle has a difficulty level from 1 to 5, with 1 being the easiest and 5 indicating the most difficult puzzles. Please take these levels with a pinch of salt; as we explained earlier, each of us finds some puzzles easier to complete than others, so this is intended as a rough guide only. It's the same for the time limit. You might whiz through certain puzzles and struggle with others. Above all, don't worry!

Keep practicing and you'll soon boost your confidence in areas you find a challenge. Develop your ability to use both sides of your upper brain, and get in touch with the mental power enjoyed by the "whole-brainers" such as Picasso, da Vinci, and Einstein.

the left/right test

Consider the statements on the following six pages. Which ones apply to you? Mark "Agree" if you feel that the statement applies. Check your responses against the list on page 14 to see whether you're predominantly a left-brain or a right-brain thinker.

AGREE

1   I love looking at maps.

2   I think I'd make a good accountant.

3   I'm usually good at remembering street names and intersections.

4   I think that, in the vast majority of cases, there's only one way to do something well.

5   I enjoy doing number puzzles.

6   I think you can often make a point more effectively with a cartoon or a diagram than in words.

7   If I've lost something, I try to picture in my head where I was and what I was doing when I last had it.

8   If I'm studying, I make bulleted lists of information points.

9   I love maze puzzles.

AGREE

10 If I needed to, I think I'd find it easy to describe in detail the appearance of someone I'd met only once.

11 I'm good at games that ask you to recognize an object from partial glimpses of it.

12 When I meet new people, I find it easier to remember them by their face and appearance rather than their name.

13 If I'm hiking in an unfamiliar landscape, I will work out where I am by looking at landmarks.

14 When I'm shopping, I like to make a mental calculation of cost before I pay.

15 If I walk into a mostly empty cinema or hall, I will usually sit on the right-hand side.

16 If someone asks for directions, I prefer to draw him or her a map rather than give detailed directions.

17 I like to imagine rearranging the furniture in my home.

AGREE

18 If I'm assembling a piece of furniture, I always follow the instructions step by step.

19 I love studying sports statistics.

20 When I'm taking notes, I prefer to draw "thought maps" and line diagrams rather than make lists.

21 I think people work best when they follow a routine step by step rather than work things out as they go along.

22 I find it easy to see how things fit together.

23 I like to draw up "To do" lists.

24 I don't like formal dances. I like responding to the flow of the music.

25 I'm bored by numbers and as a result sometimes let my finances get bungled.

26 I love doing crosswords and working out anagrams.

AGREE

27 More often than I'd like, I take what people say at face value and miss that they're being sarcastic.

28 I find that time flies when doing calculations.

29 I enjoy writing letters.

30 If I'm walking through a city I don't know, I work out which way to go by judging distance and direction.

31 After I meet new people, I'm good at remembering their eye color or the pattern of their scarf.

32 I usually find it quite easy to judge whether things will fit in a space, for example, if I'm packing or moving furniture.

33 I write a blog or diary.

34 I think I'd make a good detective—I'm good with details.

35 I love doing lateral-thinking tests.

AGREE

36 I've been complimented on my ability to put things in context.

37 I often don't know the correct names of streets and buildings even in a neighborhood with which I am familiar.

38 If I'm doing a jigsaw puzzle, I'm good at getting the overall picture and seeing how the pieces fit into it.

39 I've been complimented on creative thinking in problem-solving.

40 I'm good at picking out a friend's face in a crowd.

41 I'm good at sensing people's moods from their intonation and the way they speak.

42 On projects, I sometimes get bogged down in a task and do it more carefully and in greater detail than is required.

43 My mind's like a calculator. I've always found arithmetic easy.

AGREE

44 I love doing logical-thinking challenges.

45 I feel connected to other people and the world around me.

46 Right from school, I've found grammar and spelling easy.

47 I tend to misunderstand proverbs such as "Never change horses in midstream." I don't get the broader meaning.

48 I tend to panic if I have to make a quick calculation.

49 I'm good at judging distances.

50 I have a very good sense of direction.

Answers to the Left/Right Test

How did you respond to statements 1–50? Each time you marked Agree, you will have tended toward being either a left-brain thinker (L) or a right-brain thinker (R) as follows. Check the numbers of your marked boxes against the following list and count up the number of L (left-brain) and R (right-brain) responses to discover whether you're more of a left-brain or a right-brain thinker.

1 AGREE MEANS R, 2 AGREE MEANS L . . .

3 L	11 R	19 L	27 L	35 R	43 L
4 L	12 R	20 R	28 L	36 R	44 L
5 L	13 L	21 L	29 L	37 R	45 R
6 R	14 L	22 R	30 R	38 R	46 L
7 R	15 R	23 L	31 L	39 R	47 L
8 L	16 R	24 R	32 R	40 L	48 R
9 R	17 R	25 R	33 L	41 R	49 R
10 L	18 L	26 L	34 L	42 L	50 R

left-brain puzzles

How's your eye for detail and skill with numbers? These puzzles provide practice in activities typically associated with your upper brain's left hemisphere. You should take this path first if your score in the Left/Right Test indicated that you're stronger in typically right-hemisphere processing and mental activities.

LEVEL 5

4 MINS

The Four-Times-Fifty Grid

Successful artist Georgia took a course to develop the numerical skills she needs to keep her business accounts and other paperwork shipshape. The first task set by the teacher, Marcus, was to solve his Four-Times-Fifty Grid (opposite). He asked the students, "Can you divide the grid up into four equally sized, equally shaped parts, each containing numbers that add up to 50?"

7	7	9	9	9	9
9	4	4	4	5	5
8	8	4	1	2	6
3	2	9	5	1	7
2	8	5	8	3	7
8	7	1	5	7	2

THINKING TIP
We're working in 2D not 3D—the four parts can be rotated, but not flipped over.

Number Palette

When Winston retired from his job as an actuary, he took up watercolor painting. The pretty little palette he used in his new hobby inspired him to come up with the design (opposite) of a number-logic puzzle for his grandsons, Jordan and Nathan. The boys needed help to develop a typically left-brain facility with numbers, and Winston told them, "Look carefully and try to think logically. The circles in the left-hand palette have been rearranged in the right-hand one. They are in the same pattern, but in a different order. Can you work out their new positions from the clues given?"

- All the black circles are on the right.
- The bottom two circles add up to 7.
- The top two circles add up to 4.

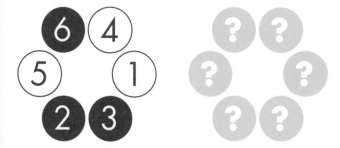

As with any test of logical thinking, here we need to proceed step by step and start by arranging the black circles on the right-hand side of the palette.

LEVEL 1
1
MIN

Anthony's Plot Box

Anthony often finds that the students in his creative-writing course benefit from practicing logical and sequential thinking, so he has them play Plot Box. This is a version of the popular children's game of boxes: Each player takes turns to join two adjacent dots with a line. If a player's line completes a box, the player wins the box and has another turn.

Opposite is a game shown after students Philippe and Natalie have been playing for several turns. Next it's Natalie's turn. Where can she draw her line to give Philippe the minimum number of boxes on his next turn?

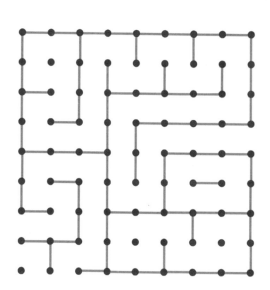

Remember that Natalie has to think one step ahead—in particular, to avoid setting up boxes that Philippe could complete with one stroke of his pen.

Hugs and Kisses

In Xavier's family, when you're signing a card, O stands for a hug just as X stands for a kiss. So he had fun working out this logic and sequence puzzle for his girlfriend Sarah. In Xavier's game, the numbered squares around the edge of the grid describe the number of crosses in all the vertical, horizontal, and diagonal lines connecting with that numbered square. Sarah's job is to complete the grid so that there is a nought (hug) or a cross (kiss) in every square. Can you help her?

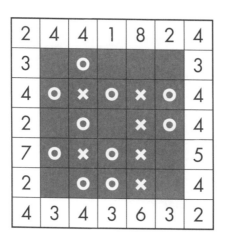

THINKING TIP

Sarah could start with the square containing 8—and should remember that a numbered square at the grid's edge can connect in two or three ways, always to a horizontal or vertical line, as well as to one or two diagonals.

LEVEL 1
1
MIN

Code Path

Saul, a mathematician and amateur historian, devised a codebreaking computer game named Code Path. The puzzle opposite is from the Time Travel level of the game, where players have to break codes to identify the names of past notables and places, as well as dates. This question asks: Which famous name can be spelled out by traveling once to each circle along the lines?

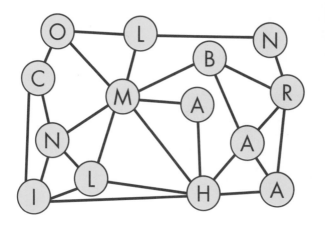

THINKING TIP

Saul is so tall that he has to have his clothes handmade. He likes to include the names of very tall people in his game—the answer here is that of a past notable who was the tallest person of his type in history.

25

LEVEL 2
3 MINS

Number Sentence

Marisa loves playing around with numbers and making sums, so she devised this magnetic board game, Number Sentence. Lightly magnetized numbers and math symbols adhere to the board: Players have to make a working sum that contains positive numbers only and fills all the spaces. She's pitching the game to some potential investors as part of a package: "Left Brain/Right Brain—Games to Balance Your Thinking." She asked them to create a sum for her, and they've presented her with this challenge. Now her brain has gone blank under pressure. Can you help Marisa create a working sum using the mathematical symbols +, −, ÷, and x? The symbols can be used in any order. Only one symbol has been used twice.

| 5 | 4 | 3 | 1 | 2 | 6 |

= 3

THINKING TIP

It helps to jot the sum down on a piece of paper and then try out different combinations of mathematical symbols to see which ones fit.

27

Order, Order

John is an actor who likes to do number puzzles such as Order, Order to focus before he goes on stage. For his current play, *Look After Number One*, typically left-brain numerical juggling is particularly appropriate, since he is playing an artist obsessed with numbers who produces large canvases covered with numerals. In John's puzzle, every row and column contains the same numbers and math signs (–, +, x), but they are arranged in a different order each time. Can you help him find the correct order to arrive at the totals shown?

4	−	1	×	2	+	3	=	9
							=	13
							=	5
							=	3
=		=		=		=		
5		7		16		19		

THINKING TIP

It may help you to take a pad and pencil, then jot down possible number combinations that produce the correct answers.

Number Ninja

Ramsey, a graffiti artist, has had the wild idea of painting sudoku grids on white walls around the city by night. Styling himself The Number Ninja, he leaves out heavy-duty markers for people to fill in the grids. Here's one of the grids he painted in the city's riverside district. As in all sudokus, your task is to fill in the empty squares so that each 3 x 3 block of nine and each vertical and horizontal line contains the numbers 1 to 9.

	8	5	7					9
						6		
	9	2					1	8
		5		1				4
		6				8		
1			9		6			
9	4					3	8	
5		3		7				
					2	9	5	

THINKING TIP

Sudoku experts recommend penciling into the grid all possible numbers for each position before firming up the number choices. Of course, anyone doing one of Ramsey's graffiti grids would have to copy the grid down first.

Allencia Letter Panel

Isaiah, a student majoring in anthropology, designed a video game in which players explore the ruins of a lost mountaintop city called Allencia. In order to enter the underground palace, they must solve the letter panel shown opposite. To complete the grid, every row, column, and outlined area must contain the letters A, B, C, D, E, and F.

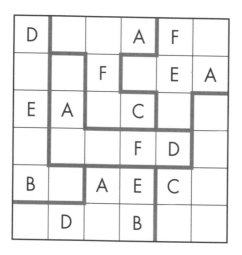

THINKING TIP

Start with the fourth column from the left, and then do the second row down. You could adapt the tip from page 31, and try penciling in possible solution letters until you eliminate them.

LEVEL 2
4
MINS

Zigzag Path

Mathematics teacher Sandeep is passionate about his subject and marks out the grid in his backyard to entertain his grandchildren, Nisha, Neela, and Arun. The object of the game is to trace a single path from the top-left corner to the bottom-right corner of the grid, traveling through all of the cells in either a horizontal, vertical, or diagonal direction. Every cell must be entered once only and the path must travel through the numbers in the sequence 1-2-3-4-5-6, 1-2-3-4-5-6, and so on. It's okay for your path to cross over itself en route. Can you help the children find their way?

1	4	3	2	1	6
2	5	6	1	2	5
3	3	4	2	4	3
4	5	2	3	1	4
6	5	6	1	6	5
1	2	3	4	5	6

THINKING TIP

As Sandeep shows the children, the first four steps are pretty clear.

LEVEL 3
3
MINS

One-Way Walk

Kevin is a successful architect who also creates puzzles for his games-mad children. This one is loosely based on a bungalow he is designing for a reclusive author. The question Kevin poses to his children is: Can you walk through every door in this design exactly once, without retracing your route? You can begin your route in any room, and it's permissible to leave the building.

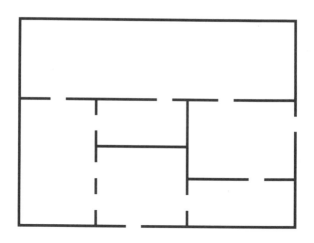

THINKING TIP
Does it help to look at the number of doors in each room?

LEVEL 2
8 MINS

Fit Figures

Can you fit the figures into the grid? One number is given to get you started.

3 DIGITS	5 DIGITS	7 DIGITS
158	~~14315~~	1268305
236	18177	2866106
595	28358	3201556
922	38756	4026958
	46384	4368022
4 DIGITS	56205	5197920
1695	68978	5845514
2826	71495	6263901
3467	87281	6312368
4094	96763	7182480
5619		7359890
7352	6 DIGITS	8031359
8904	189482	9189763
9231	245883	9367368
	874215	
	903927	

THINKING TIP

How many of the seven-digit numbers have 1 as their fifth digit?

Natalie's Plot Box

Author Natalie adapted the Plot Box challenge she learned from creative writing teacher Anthony (see Puzzle 3), and used the game in one of her private-eye stories. The story's heroine, Elle, has been captured by mob boss Christopher, who loves mathematics puzzles, and he has challenged his captive to a game. As before, each player takes turns to join two adjacent dots with a line. If a player's line completes a box, the player wins the box and has another turn. Now it's Elle's turn in this game. Where can she draw the line to give her opponent the minimum number of boxes on his next turn?

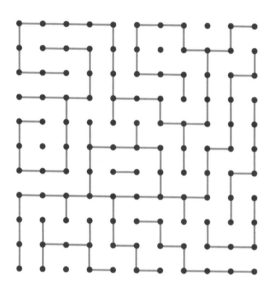

THINKING TIP
Elle needs to find a place where drawing a line will give Christopher no complete boxes, or—at worst—one box only.

LEVEL 3
6 MINS

Left Bake/Right Bake

To boost business at her bakery, which serves many scientists from a local lab, Ruby came up with a product line called Left Bake/Right Bake. Buns and cakes in the right-bake group are in unusual shapes and iced in extravagant colors. The collection of symbols opposite is an example of the left-bake line, in which symbols and numbers are iced onto cupcakes and arranged to make sums. Here, on the cakes she is placing in the window, Ruby left some symbols and figures out. Can you complete the sums? Each symbol stands for a different whole number, none being less than one. In order to reach the correct total at the end of each line, what is the value of every symbol?

$$\frac{\star}{4} + \frac{\triangle}{3} = 1 \frac{\triangle}{12}$$

$$\frac{\triangle}{2} - \frac{\star}{8} = \frac{\triangle}{\heartsuit}$$

$$\frac{\square}{49} = \frac{\triangle}{\square}$$

THINKING TIP

Each symbol stands for a whole number, but the completed sums feature fractions such as ⅓.

LEVEL 3
5
MINS

Love on a Plate

Sarah was pleased with Xavier's humorous noughts and crosses challenge (see Puzzle 4), and one day in her pottery workshop made him a version of it on a glazed plate as a return gift. As in the original, the numbered squares around the edge of the grid describe the number of crosses in all the vertical, horizontal, and diagonal lines connecting with that numbered square. Can you help Xavier complete the grid so that there is a nought or a cross in every square?

4	3	3	1	5	3	4
3						2
4				✖		3
2			✖	⭕		4
4		✖			✖	5
2				✖		3
4	2	2	3	6	4	4

THINKING TIP
Begin with the number 1, then work on the number 6 and you should be off to a flying start.

Number Sentence Launch

Marisa has found investors willing to back her Number Sentence game and the Left-Brain/Right-Brain package (see Puzzle 6). She created the number sentence shown opposite for an online promotional campaign when the package is ready for launch. As before, players have to use the mathematical symbols +, −, ÷, and x to make a working sum that contains only positive numbers and fills all the spaces provided. Only one symbol has been used twice.

| 7 | 3 | 5 | 4 | 6 | 2 |

= 22

THINKING TIP
You may want to look for a symbol that keeps the total fairly
low in the first sum in the sentence.

LEVEL 5

3
MINS

Karlheinz's Missing Note

At the back of the orchestra, Karlheinz and Dieter in the percussion section often have long periods to while away when they are not playing—so Karlheinz writes missing note puzzles for his colleague. Here is one he wrote at the Opera House last night. The position of the final note (x) is shown, but the note itself is missing. What type of note should be used—black or white, with a tail or without?

LEVEL 5
8
MINS

A Test for Sir Crispin

John shows his Order, Order game to his fellow actors backstage (see Puzzle 7), and Sir Crispin Grand, an elder statesman of the theater, asks, "Could you get me a few of these to use at Stratford, old boy?" Here is one of the puzzles John provides. As before, every row and column contains the same numbers and mathematical signs, but they are arranged in a different order each time. Can you help Sir Crispin find the correct order to arrive at the totals shown?

7	+	5	×	6	−	2	=	70
							=	14
							=	27
							=	21
=		=		=		=		
15		63		16		49		

THINKING TIP

The total is low in the first column, suggesting that the multiplication sign must come before the 2 in that calculation.

Calculation Cakes

Ruby's Left-Bake/Right-Bake line of cakes was a great success with the scientists among her clientele (see Puzzle 14), especially Tessa, who asked her to make a batch for the science laboratory's summer fête, where they would be displayed under a banner reading "Calculation Cakes." As before, each symbol stands for a different whole number, none being less than one. In order to reach the correct total at the end of each line, what is the value of every symbol?

$$\frac{\triangle}{4} - \frac{\bigstar}{\triangle} = \frac{\square}{12}$$

$$\frac{\heartsuit}{6} + 11\frac{\bigstar}{\triangle} = \heartsuit$$

$$\frac{\heartsuit}{(10 \times \bigstar) + \square} = \frac{\bigstar}{\triangle}$$

THINKING TIP

The combination of symbols in the last line suggests that the star must be a low number.

Number Stack

Retired actuary and amateur watercolorist Winston (see Puzzle 2) has devised another number-logic puzzle for his grandsons Jordan and Nathan. He added numbers to two white, two gray, and two black boxes he had left over from his art supplies. He made the arrangement (right), then posed the boys the following question: "The blocks have been rearranged. They are in the same pattern but in a different order. Can you work out their new positions from the three clues below?" Nathan and Jordan need help with this problem.

- All the blocks but one have moved.
- The bottom two blocks add up to 6, while the middle four add up to 10.
- The two black blocks are together.

5	?
6	?
1	?
4	?
2	?
3	?

THINKING TIP
Start by working out the bottom two blocks.

55

San Giovanni Letter Panel

Isaiah's video game featuring an exploration of a lost city (see Puzzle 9) was not a success, but he reworked the idea as a game searching through the imaginary modern city of San Giovanni, which has been abandoned after a climate disaster. This time players have to fill in the letter panel to gain access to medical supplies in the ruins of the city hospital. As before, your goal is to complete the grid so that each row, column, and outlined area contains the letters A, B, C, D, E, and F.

A			D		
	B				
				E	
		C			
				F	

THINKING TIP
The block containing two letters might be a good place to start.

57

Killer Sudoku

Artist Ramsey achieved notoriety with his graffiti sudokus (see Puzzle 8) and was rewarded with a contract to provide similar puzzles to appear on the walls of a city in a Hollywood movie, *Killer Sudoku*, about a number-mad serial killer. Here is one of the graffiti sudokus from the movie. As usual with a sudoku, you have to fill in the empty squares so that each 3 x 3 block of nine and each vertical and horizontal line contains the numbers 1 to 9.

		6		1	3	4		
3	1			9		6		5
		8						1
2	9					1	4	
	4	3					5	9
8					4			
9				3			1	8
		1	9	5		7		

THINKING TIP

It's all about numerical logic—go step by step. Take a break if you get stuck.

LEVEL 4
5
MINS

Zigzag Poster

Mathematics teacher Sandeep has made a second, more difficult zigzag number grid to entertain and educate his grandchildren (see Puzzle 10). He drew this one on a large poster and hung it in their playroom. As before, the object of the puzzle is to trace a single path from the top-left corner to the bottom-right corner of the grid, traveling through all of the cells in either a horizontal, vertical, or diagonal direction. Every cell must be entered once only and your path should take you through the numbers in the sequence 1-2-3-4, 1-2-3-4, and so on, and it's okay for your path to cross over itself en route. Can you find the way?

1	2	1	2	3	1	2	4
3	1	4	2	1	4	1	3
2	4	3	3	4	2	3	1
4	3	4	1	2	1	4	2
3	1	3	2	2	4	3	2
4	2	3	1	3	1	1	3
1	3	2	4	2	4	4	3
2	4	1	3	4	1	2	4

THINKING TIP

You have an advantage over Sandeep's grandchildren—you can follow the sequence of steps with the tip of your pencil even if you don't actually draw the route in.

LEVEL 2
2
MINS

Match Two

In the chic New York City hotel "The Garage," superchef Rory uses spot-the-same puzzles like this as part of a battery of games and challenges to boost quick thinking and attention to detail in his staff. This morning, he asks them, "How do these nine trucks compare? Only two are identical—can you spot the matching pair? A nice bottle of Burgundy to the winner!"

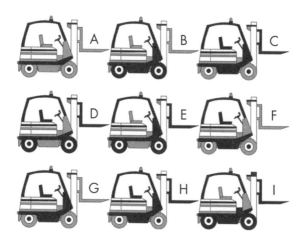

THINKING TIP

Engage left-brain processing to see the detailed differences between the trucks.

More Fit Figures

Can you fit these figures into the grid? One number is given to get you started.

3 DIGITS	5 DIGITS	7 DIGITS
380	14656	1249518
385	28360	2150959
951	40342	3309290
969	40657	3768095
	43751	4199723
4 DIGITS	45876	4406557
1037	47917	5615635
2353	52758	6839069
3171	90602	6934931
4085	94713	7336519
4116		8250325
6401	6 DIGITS	8452402
7985	575769	9553741
9678	578581	9748516
	924732	
	984336	

THINKING TIP
You have a choice of two seven-digit numbers with 1 as their second digit. Combine trial and error with logical thinking to find the next number.

right-brain puzzles

How's your spatial thinking? And your visual

awareness? These puzzles provide practice in

activities typically associated with your upper

brain's right hemisphere. You should take this

path first if your score in the Left/Right Test

indicated that you're stronger in typically left-

hemisphere processing and mental activities.

A Bit Dicey

Interior designer Bartholomew created this monochrome tile design for the wall of a games room in his client Mr. C's penthouse apartment—and a last-minute flash of inspiration made him add an odd-one-out element to the design. Presenting the finished work, he asked Mr. C, "Which of the tiles is the odd one out?"

THINKING TIP
Are the individual designs all unique?

Picture Parts

Joshua loves to see how things fit together. As a boy he was an avid modeler of boats and aircraft, and now he works as a set designer in the theater. He created this Picture Parts puzzle, inspired by his childhood love of model boats, for his niece Rosina, who is a self-styled "math geek" but wants to develop typically right-brain thinking skills. The puzzle is: Which box contains exactly the right pieces to make this picture?

THINKING TIP

You need two identical flag pieces.

Rosario's Fold and Cut

Teacher Rosario loves to use fold-and-cut puzzles, like the ones shown opposite, with her six-year-old schoolchildren to demonstrate how a small change can have major effects if it is repeated or if it is made in a particularly important place. She's made this puzzle to put on display for a parents' night in her classroom. The question is: Which of the patterns, A, B, or C, is created by this fold and cut?

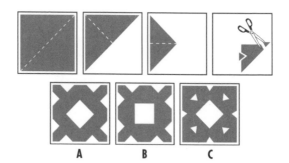

A   **B**   **C**

THINKING TIP
Will the number of incisions match the number of folds?

LEVEL 1
1
MIN

It All Fits

Art teacher Christopher uses these It All Fits puzzles as a warm-up for his students. The pieces can be assembled to make a black rectangle with the name of a famous artist on it in white. Can you mentally reconstruct it?

THINKING TIP
Jot down letters as you recognize them, starting with R.

Halfway There

Ned leads "Creativity in the Workplace" sessions. "You need to see the big picture," he tells his clients. "Don't get bogged down in the detail." He uses his Halfway There puzzle as an illustration. The half-finished picture, when complete, is symmetrical along a vertical line up the middle. By shading in every square on the left that is shaded on the right, and vice versa, a picture will emerge, but of what?

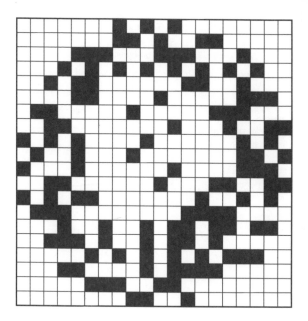

THINKING TIP
Ned teases his clients, "That shape already looks familiar."

LEVEL 2

2 MINS

Monochrome Test

Matthew called his design consultancy Monochrome, so it made sense to have all his stationery and office equipment made in black and white. He had the Monochrome Test (opposite) made up as a free game to supply in a mailing to potential clients. The test is that only one of the four sections can be found in the main grid, but which one? Beware—it may have been rotated.

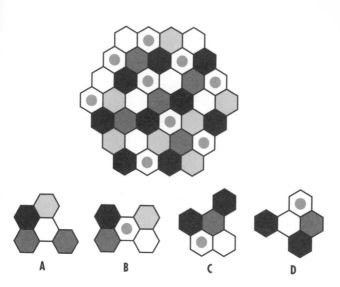

A B C D

THINKING TIP

Avoid concentrating too much on the detail of alignment of individual hexagons and try to see the combination of the pentagon groups in the main figure.

79

Devon's Honeycomb Path

Worried by declining numbers of honey bees, physics teacher Devon has begun keeping some in his small city garden. They inspired him to produce this Honeycomb Path puzzle for his students. He asks them, "Look at the progress the bee has made though the honeycomb. Where will it go next?"

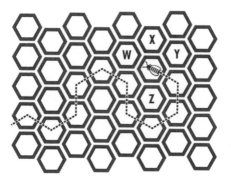

THINKING TIP

Take notice of the bee's movements in relation to the overall pattern of the honeycomb.

Piece of the Pattern

Physics lecturer Aruna began her Piece of the Pattern designs as a pastime one lonely summer break. The task here is to identify the pattern behind the placement of the shaded squares within the grid and work out which of the blocks opposite correctly fills the vacant space.

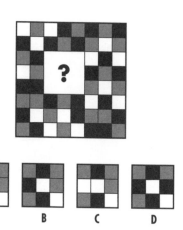

A   B   C   D

THINKING TIP
Be sure to look at the overall pattern.

Math Zone

It's time to shift perspective. Which of the four plans A–D would be the view you'd get of these four mathematical objects if you flew over in a glider? The challenge is part of a video game designed by brothers Luke and Bryan, named Math Zone, in which players explore and interact with geometric shapes in 2D and 3D.

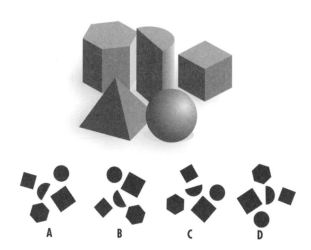

A   **B**   **C**   **D**

THINKING TIP
Take care to distinguish between the base of the pyramid and that of the square.

Put It Together

Art student Sam had the idea for this jigsaw challenge when working on his Saturday job in his uncle Fitz's automobile repair shop. He made a larger-scale drawing of a cog wheel and created ten possible pieces of the wheel as shown. Which four shapes (two black and two white) can be fit together to form the cog wheel? There's only one rule: The pieces may be rotated, but cannot be flipped over.

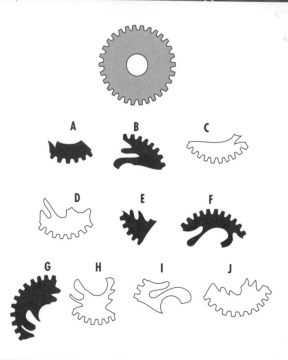

THINKING TIP

Does turning the book around in your hands help you see how the intricate inner edges of the pieces might interconnect?

A Life in Pieces

Set designer Joshua created another of his Picture Parts challenges (see Puzzle 27). He first made this design to include in the backdrop for a production of a play, *Sir Frederick Is Still at Lunch*, about a portly businessman whose life is falling apart. Afterward he made a puzzle from the design as a gift for the play's celebrated lead actor, Sir Crispin Grand. The question is: Which box contains exactly the right parts to make the picture of the businessman?

THINKING TIP
Try checking off the component parts in each set to identify the ones that are missing.

Mark the Boundaries

James, a cartographer, was inspired by his love of maps to create this Mark the Boundaries challenge for his girlfriend Maureen. She is intrigued by his mapmaking work and, in preparation for a fine art course, asks him to help her practice visualizing shapes and areas. The task in James's challenge is to cut two straight lines through the large shape to make three identical component parts. Maureen finds this really hard. Can you help her?

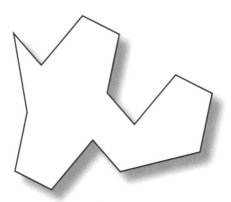

THINKING TIP
To make three identical component parts, you'll need to recreate—twice over—the sharp, V-shaped protuberance at the top of the large figure.

In the Reptile House

Isabel created a large wall painting of a snake and a lizard named "In the Reptile House" for an art-school project. As an artist, she adopts an intriguing combination of typically left-brain and typically right-brain approaches—for example, she likes to include mathematical symbols like the Venn diagram circles (opposite) and attach calculation problems to her paintings. She added an extra level to "In the Reptile House" by introducing the following puzzle: Out of 100 people surveyed, 20 have never touched a reptile, while 67 have touched a snake and 71 have touched a lizard. How many have touched both a snake and a lizard?

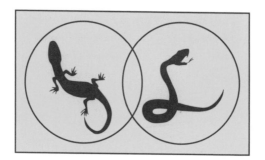

THINKING TIP
Isabel's Venn diagram design provides a simple-looking way to work out the overlap between those who have touched both a snake and lizard.

If the Name Fits

Christopher has produced another name-reconstruction challenge (see Puzzle 29) for his art students. As before, the pieces can be assembled to make a black rectangle with the name of a celebrated artist on it in white. He asks the students, "Can you reconstruct the name?"

THINKING TIP
Looks like there must be a G there.

Equidistant Four

Philosophy student Evan devised this creative-thinking challenge while working as a bartender at an elite society wedding. He challenged one of the guests, the celebrated film director Alex Sands Jr., to solve it. Here's the challenge: Four identical wine glasses are on a table. Can you find a way to position them so that the exact center of the base of each is the same distance away from the exact center of the base of all the other glasses?

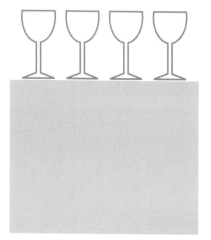

THINKING TIP

When Alex asked, "Do the glasses have to remain the same way up?" Evan shook his head almost imperceptibly.

Combination Three

Wealthy science-fiction and thriller author William V. Jones had this puzzle made up as the combination for the safe in his bedroom. Of four shapes (A–D) laid out at the bottom, three will piece together to form the top shape. When they are put in position to make the triangle, the safe opens. Which three shapes combine to make the triangle? The pieces may be rotated but must not be flipped over.

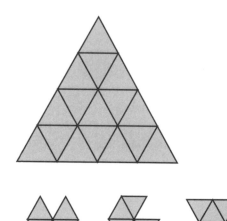

A   B   C   D

THINKING TIP
Start by deciding which shape makes up the top of the triangle.

Barely There

Ned received high approval ratings from clients attending his "Creativity in the Workplace" seminars (see Puzzle 30) and won a contract to work with the staff in the city's library department. He produced another of his Halfway There puzzles to use with a group of archivists and encouraged them to engage with typically right-brain "big-picture" processing. As before, he presented a half-finished picture that, when complete, is symmetrical along a vertical line up the middle. By shading in every square on the left that is shaded on the right, and vice versa, a picture will emerge. Can you help the librarians determine what the picture represents?

THINKING TIP

As before, the finished picture is recognizable—you'll know what it is before you finish shading the squares.

Plug the Gap

Howard, an actor trained as a mathematician, led a "Personal Growth and Creativity" course called "Whole Brain, Better Life." He devised this challenging problem for a group of mathematicians he is lecturing. At the end of a session, in which they ended up discussing the role of creativity and counterintuitive thinking in solving problems, he presented them with this image and asked, "What number should appear in the square?"

Howard told them, "Take a break. Try to get some perspective on it."

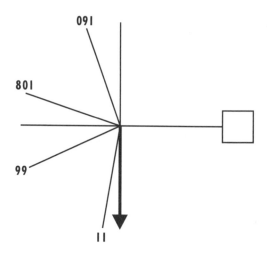

091

801

99

11

THINKING TIP
You'll need to make a creative leap for this one—consider your position?

Monochrome Fit

Matthew received many compliments on the Monochrome Test he sent out in a free mailing from his design consultancy (see Puzzle 31), so he created another similar puzzle to entertain visitors in the reception area of his downtown offices. Talented designer Rajiv has arrived for a job interview and would like to solve the puzzle before he is called in, but he is struggling to do it because he is so nervous. As before, only one of the four sections can be found in the main grid. Can you help Rajiv spot which one it is? Beware—the hidden section may not be the same way around.

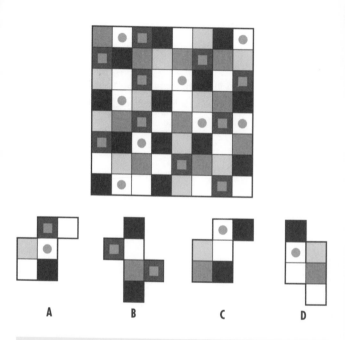

A   B   C   D

THINKING TIP
Mark or cross through each part as you rule it out. Take a break
for a few moments if you get stuck.

One into Four

James made another challenge for his girlfriend Maureen (see Puzzle 37). This time, the task is to mark three straight lines across the large shape to create four identical component parts. We know that Maureen finds these challenges pretty tough—so can you help her?

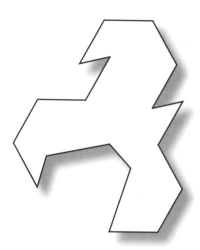

THINKING TIP

It helps to get a fresh perspective on the problem by turning the image around. You could lay a pen or pencil over the image to try out different ways of dividing it up.

Truck Parts

Sam made a second jigsaw challenge for his uncle Fitz (see Puzzle 35). This time he drew his inspiration from a truck that delivered parts to his uncle's automobile repair shop. Which six shapes (three black and three white) can be put together to form the delivery truck outline? The pieces may be rotated, but not flipped over.

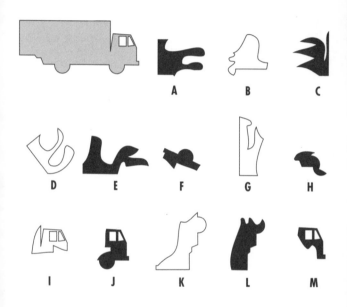

A   B   C

D   E   F   G   H

I   J   K   L   M

THINKING TIP
Start with the cab. Try to find sections that will intersect with the three possible cab pieces.

Pattern Placement

Aruna made a second of her Piece of the Pattern designs (see Puzzle 33), this time with monochrome tiles as a game for the physics faculty summer party. As before, the task is to identify the pattern behind the placement of the shaded squares within the large grid, and work out which of the blocks would correctly fill the vacant space. But now Aruna has introduced an extra level by adding numbers to the grid.

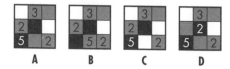

A   B   C   D

THINKING TIP
Sudoku lovers might enjoy this puzzle.

Desert Waltz

Film director Alex Sands Jr. (see Puzzle 40) asked philosophy student Evan to create a challenge about the heyday of nineteenth-century British explorers in Africa. Evan came up with the following puzzle: Hardy British explorer Sir Quentin Walsingham—known as "Waltz"—wants to cross the Yellow Desert on foot. It will take six days, but a gentleman explorer can carry only enough food and water for four days. The village in which he is staying can supply men to act as bearers, but they charge 100 shillings (the local currency) a day for their services. For the first time in his life, Sir Quentin is a little short of money. What is the smallest number of bearers he will need to help him, and what is the adventure going to cost him in local shillings? He is happy to do his share of the carrying.

THINKING TIP
Each day that passes creates room in the travelers' bags for supplies.

Domino Line

Artist Marcia devised this Domino Line image (using a bit of artistic license in her interpretation of dominoes) for the cover of a CD single called "Two Tone" released by her brother's band, The Ska Council. Subsequently she refashioned the artwork as a puzzle for the band's album, *Porkpie Hat*. The question is: What, if anything, should appear on the first domino in order to start the pattern?

THINKING TIP

Remember the title of the band's single—there may be a number clue.

Rosario's Final Fold and Cut

Teacher Rosario has made a second Fold and Cut for parents' night (see Puzzle 28), but this time the challenge is aimed at the parents themselves. This puzzle is more difficult than the one Rosario made for the children, and some of the adults struggle to complete it—which gives them more respect for their children's puzzle-solving abilities. Can you see which of the three patterns opposite is created by this fold and cut?

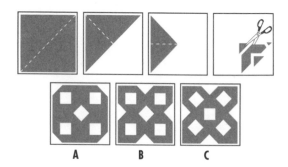

A   B   C

THINKING TIP
Consider the cut at the corner to narrow the field.

solutions

Of course, you can't have a puzzle book without an answer section. But it's worth your while making an effort not to look here too soon. If you're stumped by a puzzle, keep trying. Take a break. Come back to the problem the next day, if you like. You may be surprised by the brain's capacity to solve a problem when its attention is apparently elsewhere. You'll develop your brainpower more effectively if you find your own way to the answer.

1 The Four-Times-Fifty Grid

The completed grid looks as shown (left). As Marcus hands out the answers, he remarks that while at first we may feel frustrated with how we perform in numerical challenges like this, we all have the capacity to improve with practice. The key thing, he says, is self-belief and application: "Don't doubt that you can get better at handling numbers—think of all the other challenges you've overcome in your life."

2 Number Palette

The rearranged numbers are as shown (left). Nathan and Jordan got the solution in just over a minute. Did you manage to beat them?

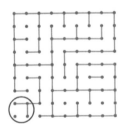

3 Anthony's Plot Box

Natalie should draw a line on the left or bottom of the square marked, since this will give up only one box to Philippe.

2	4	4	1	8	2	4
3	O	O	X	O	X	3
4	O	X	O	X	O	4
2	X	O	O	X	O	4
7	O	X	O	X	X	5
2	X	O	O	X	O	4
4	3	4	3	6	3	2

4 Hugs and Kisses

The completed grid should appear as shown. A puzzle such as this provides good practice in typically left-brain linguistic and mathematical activities, since it combines counting with the logical thought required to plot Xs and Os in the grid. Sarah is a potter and feels the need to do more thinking of this type, while Xavier—who works in insurance—is completely at home with numbers.

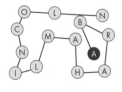

5 Code Path

The answer is Abraham Lincoln, the 16th U.S. president (1861–65). Reputedly, he stood 6 ft. 4 in. (1.93 m) in his socks, and so is the tallest U.S. president in history.

$5 \times 4 - 3 + 1 \div 2 - 6$
$= 3$

6 Number Sentence

Marisa comes up with the answer shown. Like this book, the game package she is trying to launch would offer people the chance to "balance" their thinking and improve their overall mental performance.

4	–	1	×	2	+	3	=	9
+		+		–		+		
3	×	4	–	1	+	2	=	13
×		×		+		×		
1	+	2	×	3	–	4	=	5
–		–		×		–		
2	×	3	–	4	+	1	=	3
=		=		=		=		
5		7		16		19		

7 Order, Order

John's puzzle looks like this (left) when completed. His aim is to get his whole brain active before he attempts to embody his mathematically obsessed artist. As well as doing typically left-brain number challenges such as Order, Order, he also sings and develops intuitive jazz dance movements in the green room backstage in an effort to engage his right brain.

6	8	5	7	1	4	2	3	9
3	1	4	2	9	8	6	7	5
7	9	2	6	5	3	4	1	8
2	3	9	5	8	1	7	6	4
4	5	6	3	2	7	8	9	1
1	7	8	9	4	6	5	2	3
9	4	7	1	6	5	3	8	2
5	2	3	8	7	9	1	4	6
8	6	1	4	3	2	9	5	7

8 Number Ninja

The completed grid should look as shown (left). Sudoku puzzles make you think numerically, visually, and critically all at once, so they are good for building connections between brain cells. Most of the work is done in the typically left-brain activities of processing numbers and sequences, and in logic.

D	E	B	A	F	C
C	B	F	D	E	A
E	A	D	C	B	F
A	C	E	F	D	B
B	F	A	E	C	D
F	D	C	B	A	E

9 Allencia Letter Panel

The completed grid appears as shown (left). This puzzle provides practice in typically left-brain linguistic work, manipulating and sequencing letters. When the players in Isaiah's game complete the task correctly, a palace guardian appears and shows them a secret entrance to the royal complex.

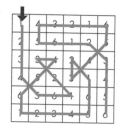

10 Zigzag Path

The correct route along the zigzag path is as shown (left). In this case, Neela finds the correct route before her siblings: She is advanced in mathematics, and Sandeep is proudly looking forward to seeing her make progress in his area of expertise. The puzzle engages typically left-brain processing involving plotting a sequence and handling numbers.

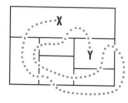

11 One-Way Walk

Yes, you can complete the route. For example, starting and finishing at X and Y (or at Y and X), you can walk through every door once. Rooms X and Y have an odd number of doors.

12 Fit Figures

The completed grid is shown (left). As you now know, complex thinking involves many parts of the brain working together, but the left hemisphere of your upper brain takes the lead in this kind of numerical processing. The puzzle is called Fit Figures because it is devised by a personal trainer, Caitlin, who is also a math tutor. She says, "The brain is like a muscle that needs regular exercise."

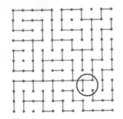

13 Natalie's Plot Box

Elle should draw her line on the right or bottom of the square marked with a circle: This will give one box only to Christopher.

14 Left Bake/Right Bake

In Ruby's arrangement, star = 3, triangle = 1, heart = 8, and square = 7, so the first line reads $\frac{3}{4} + \frac{1}{3} = 1\frac{1}{12}$. The scientists among Ruby's clientele are wowed by the Left Bake/Right Bake line and, impressed by the difficulty of the sums she included, they force Ruby to admit that she studied mathematics at college before she got into catering.

15 Love on a Plate

4	3	3	1	5	3	4
3	✗	O	O	O	✗	2
4	O	O	O	✗	O	3
2	✗	O	✗	O	O	4
4	O	✗	O	✗	✗	5
2	O	O	O	✗	✗	3
4	2	2	3	6	4	4

The completed grid is as shown (left). As explained on page 107, Xavier works with numbers every day, so he is strong in this type of typically left-brain numerical processing. At the same time, under Sarah's influence, he is trying to develop typically right-brain strengths by doing puzzles like those in the second section of the book, which test visual awareness and the capacity to see the combination of component parts in the whole.

$$\boxed{7} - \boxed{3} \times \boxed{5} \div \boxed{4} + \boxed{6} \times \boxed{2}$$
$$= \boxed{22}$$

16 Number Sentence Launch

The correct number sentence is shown. One of the beauties of math is that its symbols have meaning regardless of order. In language, words have meaning only when carefully ordered. In Marisa's game, the answer is already provided, thus limiting your choices for arranging the symbols.

17 Karlheinz's Missing Note

A note is black if it's on a space and white if it's on a line; it has a tail if it's lower than the previous note and no tail if it's higher. Therefore, the final note should be black with no tail.

18 A Test for Sir Crispin

7	+	5	×	6	−	2	=	70
×		+		−		+		
2	×	6	−	5	+	7	=	14
−		−		+		×		
5	−	2	×	7	+	6	=	27
+		×		×		−		
6	+	7	×	2	−	5	=	21
=		=		=		=		
15		63		16		49		

John's completed grid should look as shown (left). Sir Crispin Grand is particularly interested because he has just discovered "brain-training" books and games and has been told that doing mathematical calculations is especially good for building connections between brain cells, boosting your overall mental performance.

19 Calculation Cakes

In Ruby's arrangement for Tessa, triangle = 3, star = 2, square = 1, and heart = 14, so line 1 reads $\frac{3}{4} - \frac{2}{3} = \frac{1}{12}$. This kind of puzzle is a good workout for typically left-brain processing involved in mental calculations and logical deduction.

20 Number Stack

The correct arrangement is as shown (left). Winston is pleased that the two boys' facility with numbers is clearly improving.

6
2
3
4
1
5

21 San Giovanni Letter Panel

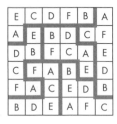

The completed grid as featured in Isaiah's climate disaster video game is as shown (left). Isaiah calls his puzzle "sudoku with letters" and his panel certainly provides the same combination of tests for your processing skills and critical thinking as a conventional sudoku puzzle.

5	8	6	7	1	3	4	9	2
3	1	7	4	9	2	6	8	5
4	2	9	8	6	5	3	7	1
2	9	5	3	8	7	1	4	6
1	6	8	5	4	9	2	3	7
7	4	3	6	2	1	8	5	9
8	5	2	1	7	4	9	6	3
9	7	4	2	3	6	5	1	8
6	3	1	9	5	8	7	2	4

22 Killer Sudoku

The completed grid is as shown. As an artist who is also a math enthusiast, Ramsey is a living example of a balanced brain in action, combining typically right-brain spatial and visual work with typically left-brain numerical processing. He argues that we boost the connections in the brain and so benefit our thinking when we try new activities. His advice is to attempt something you're not accustomed to doing at least once a week—even at the simple level of taking a different route to work, listening to an unfamiliar type of music, or buying a different newspaper.

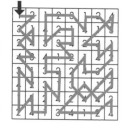

23 Zigzag Poster

The correct path is as shown (left). This time Nisha outperforms her sister Neela and is first to trace the path through the grid. Sandeep congratulates her, not only on her achievement but on her commitment in sticking at things that do not come naturally.

127

24 Match Two

The two identical forklift trucks are C and H.
Rory finds that his staff work more quickly and
harmoniously under pressure if he provides a
mental warm-up at the start of the day. Today
"The Prof," a physics student named Dylan
who is employed as a dishwasher, wins the
challenge and the bottle of Burgundy.

25 More Fit Figures

The completed grid is as shown (left). This is
another puzzle produced by Caitlin (see page
109). "We all accept that we need regular
physical exercise to keep the body in shape,"
she tells her clients. "We also need regular
mental exercise. I recommend working with
numbers and doing sudokus or even simple
calculations as fast as you can."

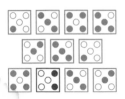

26 A Bit Dicey

The second tile from the left in the bottom
row is the odd one out (as shown on the left),
because it doesn't have a matching partner.
Each of the others can be paired up with an
identical die. Mr. C grew up on the "mean
streets," where he played dice for money. He
got the answer in under a minute.

C

27 Picture Parts

Box C is the correct answer, as shown. Rosina has a great eye for detail but found it quite a challenge to visualize how the pieces fit together.

A

28 Rosario's Fold and Cut

The correct answer is A. Rosario explains that these puzzles boost her pupils' visualization skills. A number of parents expressed interest, so Rosario devised a Fold and Cut for them to test their own skills (see Puzzle 50).

29 It All Fits

The name is that of the French Impressionist painter (Pierre-Auguste) Renoir—or, just possibly, as one of the students says, that of his son (Jean) Renoir, the filmmaker and author. Christopher likes to bombard his students with puzzles of different types, combining visual and symmetry puzzles with math challenges.

30 Halfway There

The picture is of a Number 8 pool ball (left). In college, Ned and his best friend Frank were champion players of billiards. The point with this puzzle, Ned says, is not to fill in all the squares meticulously but to use your intuition and powers of visualization to jump to a conclusion about what the image represents.

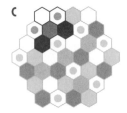

C

31 Monochrome Test

The answer is C (rotated 180°), as shown. This puzzle provides a stern test of your ability to visualize shapes in different alignments. Matthew was delighted by the response to his mailing. Three new clients made contact and later signed major contracts.

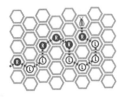

32 Devon's Honeycomb Path

Cell X is next. The pattern goes: Turn right x 1, left x 2, right x 3, left x 4, so the next move will be the first of five right turns. Devon tells his students that puzzles like these help them develop their concentration and typically right-brain discernment of how parts of the honeycomb fit into the whole.

B

33 Piece of the Pattern

Each row and column should have three black, two white, and three gray squares, so block B is the missing piece. The ability to recognize patterns is an aspect of "big-picture" right-brain functioning.

B

34 Math Zone

The answer is B, as shown. Brothers Luke and Bryan developed the Math Zone game because they wanted a project that taxed their intelligence and combined their interests—Luke is a mathematics tutor, while Bryan works in poster design at a video company. Of the two, Bryan is stronger in typically right-brain visualization. He takes any opportunity he can to improve this skill, as he finds it increases his ability to see things afresh or from an intriguing and engaging perspective when he is sketching and painting.

35 Put It Together

The four pieces are B, D, F, and I, as shown. The puzzle is another chance to develop typically right-brain skills in visualizing how parts fit together to make the whole.

131

36 A Life in Pieces

The answer is box A. Sir Crispin (see also Puzzle 18) is very pleased. He is now reading about left-brain/right-brain theory and he wants to do typically right-brain visualization challenges to balance his thinking.

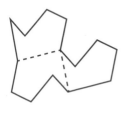

37 Mark the Boundaries

The two lines Maureen needs to draw are shown (left). Although Maureen struggled to complete this challenge, James urged her to keep trying. "Visualization skills of this sort come naturally to some people," he said, "but for others they demand practice." She is grateful for his help and on his birthday buys him a huge jigsaw puzzle of a map of the United States. "Now we'll be able to work on seeing how the parts fit into the whole," he said, rubbing his hands.

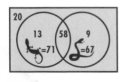

38 In the Reptile House

People who have touched a snake only: 100 − 20 − 71 = 9; People who have touched a lizard only: 100 − 20 − 67 = 13; People who have touched both: 100 − 20 − 9 − 13 = 58.

39 If the Name Fits

The name is that of French artist (Edgar) Degas. One of Christopher's students, Jolene, comments that after doing visualization puzzles like this she sees things in a fresh light. "They spur my creativity," she says.

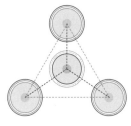

40 Equidistant Four

Place three glasses the right way up in an equilateral triangle with the center of the bases one glass height apart. Place the fourth glass upside down in the center of the triangle. Alex couldn't work it out, but chuckled with delight when Evan showed him the solution. "I like it," he murmured, "that's some creative thinking."

41 Combination Three

The three are A, C, and D, as shown. In one of Jones's detective novels, criminal locksmith and amateur Egyptologist Walter J. Walter used the design to form a pyramid in a security device guarding a strong room. Walter's foe, artist-turned-detective M. Paul Albert, used his well-developed eye for visual patterns to break the code and find the goods.

42 Barely There

The completed picture is of a bear. This puzzle requires you to use your visual imagination to create a new perspective on a scene, which also boosts your right-brain processing.

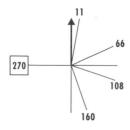

43 Plug the Gap

The number in the box should be 270. If you turn the diagram upside down, it becomes a chart with the bearings 11, 66, 108, and 160 degrees marked on it. Howard remarks that the puzzle requires a degree of lateral thinking to see the need to turn the image upside down, and this engages the typically right-brain processing of seeing the numbers in their context. The final part, working out the sequence of the numbers, requires typically left-brain processing, making the puzzle a test for the whole brain.

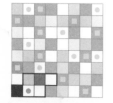

44 Monochrome Fit

The answer is D (rotated 90°), as shown. The right brain is engaged in working out the spatial and pattern relationships between the small pieces and the main design.

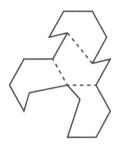

45 One into Four

The three lines Maureen needed to create four identical parts are as shown (left). James decided he liked the energy of the overall design—something like a winged bird, he felt—and decided to adopt it as a logo for his mapmaking business, Point to Point.

46 Truck Parts

Parts B, G, I (white), and E, F, L (black) combine to make the truck outline as shown (left). Sam created the puzzle in wood at art school and presented it to Uncle Fitz—this time as a Christmas gift. Uncle Fitz put both puzzles out on the counter in the garage office where customers wait to pay.

A

47 Pattern Placement

The missing piece is A, as shown (left). Each row and column contains one white, five gray, and two black squares, and numbers that total 10. At the physics faculty summer party, Aruna explains some of the background to the theory of left-brain/right-brain functioning to her colleague, Dr. Baird. She tells him that typically right-brain processing controls the combining of parts in the whole, as in this puzzle, and making sense of the parts in context. "We use this type of processing," she says, "when we recognize the combination of eyes, nose, mouth, cheeks, and chin as a person's face."

48 Desert Waltz

Sir Quentin needs two bearers. The first one walks for a day, then returns home, having given one day's supply of food and water to each of the other two travelers. The second goes for one more day, then returns home having given Sir Quentin two days' food and water. Sir Quentin now has the four days' supply he needs to complete the trip. This amounts to two days' round trip for the first bearer, four days for the second. Sir Quentin will need to find 600 shillings to pay the bearers' fees.

49 Domino Line

The first domino should have ½ on top and
have one spot on the bottom. There are two
arithmetical series (1, 2, 3, 4, 5 and ½, 1, 2,
4, 8) appearing in zigzag from left to right.
Marcia believes she is stronger in right-brain
processing: She can see the how the spots form
a pattern but finds it hard to explain clearly
why. On the strength of their album (and its
acclaimed cover), The Ska Council was hired
as house band at a new club, and Marcia
designed their stage set.

50 Rosario's Final Fold and Cut

B

The answer is B. Rosario prepared a special
presentation explaining that this kind of
thinking challenge develops the children's
ability to see and intuit connections, and to
understand the importance of context. Fold and
Cut puzzles also bring home to the children the
multiplying effects of a person's actions.

further reading

The Brain That Changes Itself: Stories of Personal Triumph from the Frontiers of Brain Science by Norman Doidge. Penguin Books, 2008

Climbing the Blue Mountain by Eknath Easwaran. Nilgiri Press, 1996

Happiness Hypothesis: Putting Ancient Wisdom to the Test of Modern Science by Jonathan Haidt. Arrow Books, 2007

Meditation and Modern Psychology by Robert E. Ornstein. Malor Books, 2008

My Stroke of Insight by Jill Bolte Taylor. Hodder Paperbacks, 2009

Passage Meditation by Eknath Easwaran. Nilgiri Press, 2008

The Plastic Mind by Sharon Begley. Constable, 2009

The Right Mind: Making Sense of the Hemispheres by Robert E. Ornstein. Harcourt Brace International, 1998

What Makes a Champion! by Allan Snyder. Penguin Books Australia, 2002

CHARLES PHILLIPS is the author of more than 20 books, including *Brain Box*, *Memory Booster*, and the *How to Think* series of six puzzle books. He is a contributor to more than 25 other titles, including *The Reader's Digest Compendium of Puzzles & Brain Teasers* (2001), and is a keen collector of games and puzzles.

Puzzle Compilers: David Bodycombe, Guy Campbell, Puzzle Press, Probyn Puzzles
Page 113: iStockphoto.com/Naci Yavuz

COLLECT THESE FUN PUZZLES
IN THE POCKET POSH® SERIES!

Sudoku
Killer Sudoku
Easy Sudoku
Large Print Sudoku
London Sudoku
New York Sudoku
San Francisco Sudoku
Christmas Sudoku
Christmas Easy Sudoku
Girl Sudoku
Hanukkah Sudoku
Thomas Kinkade Sudoku
Thomas Kinkade Sudoku
    with Scripture
Shopaholic's Sudoku
Sudoku & Beyond
Code Number Sudoku
Sudoku Fusion
Wonderword™
Word Roundup™
Word Roundup™
    Hollywood
Large Print Word
    Roundup™
Christmas Word
    Roundup™
Word Roundup™
    Challenge
Christmas Word
    Roundup™ Challenge
Crosswords
Christmas Crosswords
Easy Crosswords
Girl Crosswords
Hanukkah Crosswords

Thomas Kinkade
    Crosswords
Thomas Kinkade
    Crosswords with
    Scripture
New York Crosswords
Jumble® Crosswords
Jumble® BrainBusters
Double Jumble®
Bible Jumble®
Word Search
Girl Word Search
WORDScrimmage™
Left Brain/Right Brain
Logic
Christmas Logic
Hangman
Girl Hangman
Hidato®
Mazematics
Sukendo®
Brain Games
Christmas Brain Games
Codewords
One-Minute Puzzles
Jane Austen Puzzles
    & Quizzes
William Shakespeare
    Puzzles & Quizzes
Charles Dickens
    Puzzles & Quizzes
Irish Puzzles & Quizzes
London Puzzles
    & Quizzes

J. R. R. Tolkien Puzzles
    & Quizzes
Sherlock Holmes
    Puzzles & Quizzes
King James Puzzles
Petite Pocket Posh®
    Sudoku
Petite Pocket Posh®
    Crosswords
Petite Pocket Posh®
    Word Roundup™
Word Puzzles
Mom's Games to Play
    with Your Kids
    (Ages 4–6 & 7–12)
Cryptograms
Almost Impossible
    Number Puzzles
Almost Impossible
    Word Puzzles
Word Lover's Puzzle
    & Quiz Book
Lateral Thinking
The New York Times
    Brain Games
Quick Thinking
Logical Thinking
Memory Games
Cat Lover's Puzzle
    & Quiz Book
Creative Thinking
Unolingo
Tactical Thinking
Word Clue Sudoku